Preschool Phonics
Single letter sounds

By Lauren Benzaken

For Leah.

Contents

Introduction

I have always had a strong interest in how children develop and learn — an interest that, just over a decade ago, led me to a degree in Childhood Culture and Education and, subsequently, to completing a PGCE (the UK's teaching qualification). However, although I have found myself in a number of educational roles over the past ten years — ranging from traditional classroom teacher, to face-to-face private tutor, to intervention specialist — it has only been since having my own daughter that I have been able to experience a child's development from day one, and this has given me a fresh perspective on life and education.

I am writing this in July 2020, and, over the past few months, the world has changed irrevocably due to Covid-19. I — like many parents around the world — have had to embrace homeschooling. And at the outset of this new learning regimen, I knew I wanted to utilise the extra time with my three-year-old child to focus on Phonics learning. Maintaining the attention of your own child is nothing like teaching a classroom of children, or even like intervention work. I knew that I needed to find ways of keeping my daughter engaged in order to ensure we could develop a routine that would enable her to build up her learning and knowledge each day. To do this, we would play games, explore books and, of course, do as much repetition as possible, in as many different ways as was possible. I soon realised that, despite there being many fantastic resources out there, I couldn't find one that enumerated the steps a parent needed to take to develop a child's phonics learning prior to formal school enrolment — so I created one myself.

On the next few pages I discuss what I call "pre-formal phonics experiences" — which refers to activities you can do with your child to help ready them for the contents of this book — plus instructions on how to use this book. There are many children who are ready to start learning before they commence school, and this guide gives you the tools to prepare your child for their learning journey. I am also hopeful that, aside from helping your child learn all about single letter sounds (and equipping you with the tools to teach them), this book can also be used when your child begins formal education — and can function to supplement and scaffold the phonics learning that is undertaken in schools.

You will notice throughout the book that I mention particular resources that can be used alongside my suggested activities, and I have made these available to download for free at the following URL:

https://accoladetuition.com/phonics1-resources

Pre 'Formal' Phonics

Before moving onto formal letter identification, children in nurseries (and organically at home) go through different pre-phonics experiences that prepare them to eventually associate sounds (phonemes) with written letters (graphemes). These experiences revolve around speaking and listening activities such as:

- Exploring environmental sounds: Being able to identify different sounds in their environment and what they are associated with. An example of this is when we go to a farm with a child, or read them a farm story, and explore animal sounds in the process. Another example is babies and toddlers associating the sound of a doorbell with someone coming to visit. This is then transported to their play, during which they might act out real life scenarios they have experienced.
- Experimenting with sounds: Playing with instruments and using their voices to experiment with making loud/quiet and high/low sounds.
- Rhythm: Exploring rhythm through song, dance and body percussion.
- Rhyme: This can be explored during conversations, but I often find that rhymes crop up most when reading books and discussing the sounds that make up different words.
- Oral segmenting and blending: An adult saying "look at the c-a-t [sounds out the word]" and a child putting/blending together the sounds to say "cat". Although this can be taught prior to letter identification, I do find it is consolidated most when we actually explore letters. At any rate, it is covered in the activities suggested later on in this book.

Here are some ideas of activities you can do with your child to help them fine-tune their speaking and listening skills, hone their understanding of sounds, and develop their attention span:

Listening Walks: When you are out and about, discuss what sounds you can hear around you. This can be done when sitting in the park, driving in the car, or walking around a shopping centre or high street. Encourage your child to talk about what makes different sounds and to describe sounds using vocabulary associated with volume and pitch ('loud', 'quiet', 'high', 'low'), and distance ('near', 'far').

Initial Sound Identification: This is an activity that you will be working on for each new sound we learn in this book; however, I recommend trying to enact this in your everyday life, too. When cooking a meal you can say "tonight we are having spaghetti — spaghetti starts with a 's' sound"; or "it's time for a 'b', 'b', bath".
Eventually your child will pick up on identifying initial sounds in words. You could also

do this during bedtime reading by pointing out initial sounds in key words (though don't overdo this as you want to keep the flow of the story!).   "b-b-bath"

Follow the Leader: This can be used when exploring sounds as well as rhythm. Say a word in a loud/quiet/low/high voice and ask your child to repeat this back in the same voice. Alternatively, ask your child to be the leader, then you copy what they say. In terms of body percussion, create a sequence of body sounds — such as 'clap', 'clap', 'stamp', 'stamp', 'stamp' — and invite your child to repeat what you have done. Again, take turns being the leader.

Refrains and Rhymes: We all know it is of the utmost importance to read to your child, and that it is best to start a 'reading routine' from infancy. When they are babies, it is great to read sound books; but, as they get older (from around the age of 2), it is really important to incorporate books that contain repetitive language that will allow your child to join in and explore rhythm. As well as books with repetitive language, it is very beneficial to read books that contain lots of rhyming words. My daughter loves joining in with all these books during bedtime reading, and it is a great opportunity to extend your child's ability to find words that rhyme.

Singing and Dancing: Music naturally develops a child's ability to follow rhythm and allows for opportunities to explore sound and rhyme. When dancing, a child can work on following routines which helps improve their attention as well as creating sequences. I have always tried to make up little funny songs and rhymes about things we are doing. For example, when it's time for bed, I might sing something like, "it's time for bath and bed, it's time for bed and bath, oh yay, oh yay, oh yay, it's time for bath and bed" to the tune of 'The Farmer in the Dell'; or I may just randomly start coming up with words (real and nonsensical) that rhyme with something we are playing with — puzzle, muzzle, fuzzle, duzzle. Kids will pick up on these little games and do them spontaneously themselves.

Initial Sound Activities

Below is a list of some activities to help your child practise and consolidate the new sounds they learn (though of course more activities still will be presented throughout the book!). I have split them up into two types of activities – 'Anywhere, Any Time' activities, and others that require some preparation and basic resources. The 'Anywhere, Any Time' activities are great because you can do them in the car, when on a walk, before bed time, during bath time... Literally anywhere and at any time!

Anywhere, Any Time Activities

Ping-Pong Words: Choose a sound to practise and then take turns saying words that begin with that sound. The aim is to think of as many words as possible without repeating a word someone has already said. You could adapt this activity by using certain themes i.e. animals that begin with 'w' - and this game can of course be played with two or more players.

 I Spy: You or your child says "I spy with my little eye something beginning with..." and then either the sound or name of the letter, and the other participant/s need to guess what you had been looking at.

Letter Walk: When you are out and about with your child, encourage them to look for different letters on shop signs, house fronts, car number plates, street signs, and so on (consolidating both the letter sound and its name as you do so).

 Sound Hunt: Choose a sound and ask your child to go around the house looking for objects beginning with that sound.

Minimal Prep, Basic Resources Activities

Letter Poster: Create a poster to go with each new letter learnt. Draw different things that begin with that sound or cut and paste pictures from magazines. You could also hunt for that letter in magazines and create a collage of the different sizes and fonts you find.

 **Sorting by Sounds:** Collect objects/pictures and ask your child to sort them on the basis of what sound they begin with. Begin with two sounds; you can then push your child by introducing further objects and asking them to sort them into three or more sounds.

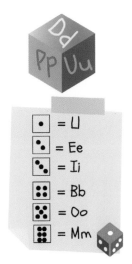

Roll A Sound: Using the dice template provided in the resource link, write different letters on each section. Take turns rolling the dice and say the sound of the letter you land on. Alternatively, you could use an ordinary dice, and create a 'rule sheet' where you assign sounds to numbers: for instance, 1 dot = 's', 2 dots = 't', and so forth. This is great if you do not have the resources needed to create a dice and also allows your child to cover two learning objectives in one go, since you will also be demonstrating what is known as 'number pattern recognition' — that is, understanding that, for instance, four dots equates to the number four.

Speed Sounds: Using the sound cards in the link provided, show your child one sound at a time, asking them to name each sound they see. I like to make two piles when doing this — one pile with all the cards my daughter got right, and one with the ones she said incorrectly or didn't know. When we are done going through the stack of sounds, we go over the ones she didn't know/said incorrectly.

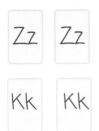

Snap: Print two lots of the sound cards provided in the link. You can begin by getting your child to match the pairs together or just recapping each sound and talking about things that begin with each sound and how each letter is formed (written). Then move onto playing 'Snap'; but instead of shouting "SNAP!" when you get a pair that is the same, shout out the letter name or sound.

Notes:

- Although I encourage parents to introduce the letter name for each letter as you go through the book, it is important that the main focus remains on the sounds of each letter when talking about words and objects. For example, when posed with the question 'What animals or objects can you think of that begin with 'a'?' we are talking about the sound the letter 'a' makes, not its name — the sound in 'ant' as opposed to 'Asian elephant'.

- Many parents feel inclined to teach their child the capital letters of the alphabet before the lowercase ones. However, in schools and nurseries, children are introduced to the lowercase letters when presented with phonics. I have set out this book to have the uppercase and lowercase letters side by side as I wanted children to make the connection between both letters. In truth, aside from the letters at beginning of names, shops, and so forth, most of the text children will see around them will be in lowercase form. When reading stories at bedtime, your child will see more lowercase than uppercase letters, giving you opportunities to recap the learning you have covered.

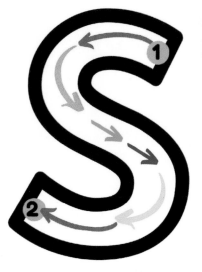 

Introduce the name of the letter and the sound it makes, like in the word 'scorpion'.

<u>s</u>corpion

Encourage your child to use their finger to trace over the 's' as they say it. You should talk about what the letter looks like and could make up a little phrase, such as "slide down the s".

The <u>s</u>nake <u>s</u>lithered in the <u>s</u>oft <u>s</u>oil and then <u>s</u>lid off down the <u>s</u>loping hill.

List all the 's' words after you read the sentence above to your child.

Which of these begin with <u>s</u>?

seahorse   **blue whale**   **dog**   **salamander**

Talk about the initial sound of each word/picture. You might need to model this for the first few letters in the book.

What animals or objects can you think of that begin with <u>s</u>?

6

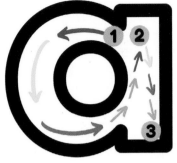

anteater

As with 's', encourage your child to trace over the letter 'a'. I have used grey arrows to show your child when they need to pick up their finger. You may want to say: "first you draw the top of a triangle, then you lift your finger and draw a line across the middle".

Alligators get very angry when their prey manages to avoid their amazing, mighty jaws.

Which of these begin with a?

alpaca   **clown fish**   **cow**   **ant**

What animals or objects can you think of that begin with a?

Encourage your child to look around them for anything that begins with a given sound. You could also name people you know.

Segmenting & Blending

From here onwards, you will see decodable words at the bottom of each letter page (these are words that can be broken down phonetically and blended back together). Your child may not be ready for this just yet, but you could model how to say each sound in a word and then blend all the sounds together. Emphasise how we read from left to right using your finger, pointing to each sound as you say it; then go back to the beginning and swipe across the blended word e.g. "b-a-t, bat".

Can you find a...: This is a really simple activity - basically just try to incorporate blending into your every day life. For example, when setting the table, you could ask your child to get a 'sp-oo-n'. You are not always necessarily splitting a word into its individual sounds, but working on your child just blending two or three parts together to get them to improve their blending ability. You can make this more of a game by using a doll, soft toy or puppet and explain that it can only talk in sounds (or can only use sounds for some words).

c-a-t

Extended I Spy: The game of 'I Spy' can be adapted in order to practise blending words — you can say "I spy with my little eye a c-a-t" and your child needs to blend the sounds together. Equally, your child can practise segmenting (taking words apart) by being the one saying "I spy..." To augment your child's learning you may want to have a group of items ready to 'spy', especially if you have a sound you want to focus on.

Clap the Sounds: This activity focuses on segmenting words first and then blending. You provide your child with a word (say it orally) such as 'dog', or a picture of a dog. They then break the word into its sounds 'd-o-g', clapping each part, and then repeat the word as a whole. This will prepare your child for when they move onto reading, as they will need to be able to first sound out (segment) a word before blending the sounds together. If clapping doesn't work, you could use an elastic band on your child's hands. They stretch the band for each sound and then snap back, 'pushing' all the sounds together.

tarantula

Say the t sound as you follow the arrows

The **t**remendous **t**iger took no **t**ime in catching his **t**asty food.

Which of these begin with t?

fish **toad** **goat** **turkey**

What animals or objects can you think of that begin with t?

Look out for the footprint words from this page onwards.

For the word 'sat' (and all decodeable words) you should say the sounds slowly: s-a-t. Repeat it a couple of times before speeding up, so it sounds more like a blended word.

Write a letter with chalk on the ground or on a large piece of paper (basically create a 'track') and your child could trace over this using a toy car, horse or small ball.

parrot

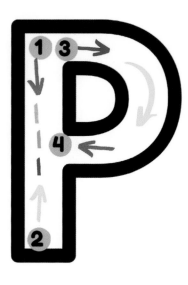

The pretty peacock particularly enjoys prancing around the children's playground.

Which of these begin with p?

polar bear

butterfly

hen

panda

What animals or objects can you think of that begin with p?

pat

tap

sap

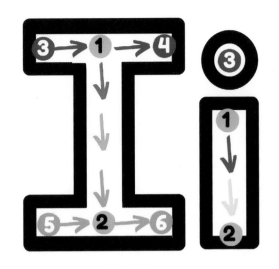

Follow the numbers when tracing but lift twice, once after the colourful arrows and again after the dark grey ones.

insects

Inchworms move **i**ncredibly slowly as they **i**nch forwards **i**n the direction of food.

Which of these begin with **i**?

dragonfly   impala   iguana   shrimp

What animals or objects can you think of that begin with **i**?

pit   it   pip   sit   tip

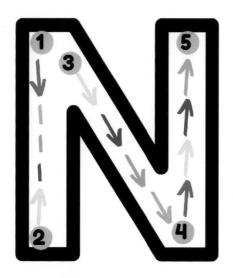 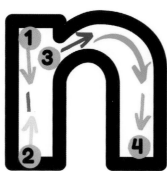 

narwhal

Say the n sound as you follow the arrows

 The narrow newt moved nimbly across the newly painted navy wall leaving neat newt footprints.

Which of these begin with n?

llama numbat rattlesnake nightingale

What animals or objects can you think of that begin with n?

pan tan pin tin nap

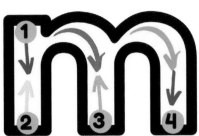

<u>m</u>osquito

 <u>M</u>any <u>m</u>oths are nocturnal which means they <u>m</u>ostly come out when the <u>m</u>oon is shining at night.

Which of these begin with <u>m</u>?

  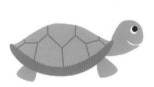 

monkey   **hummingbird**   **tortoise**   **meerkat**

What animals or objects can you think of that begin with <u>m</u>?

I will point out to my daughter when we see a word with a capital letter and explain that capital letters are used at the beginning of names.

 **am**   **man**   **map**   **mat**    **Sam**

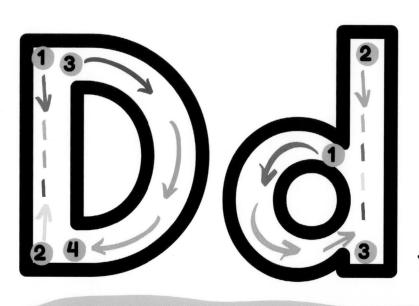

donkey

Say the d sound as you follow the arrows

 The **d**elightful **d**almatian puppy had **d**ozens of **d**inky black **d**ots.

Which of these begin with d?

dove   pig   swan   deer

What animals or objects can you think of that begin with **d**?

did   dip   sad   dad   and

The letter 'g' makes two sounds:
soft 'g' (j sound) = when 'g' is followed by e, i or y.

gerbil

hard 'g' (g sound) = when 'g' is followed by any other letter.

goat

The greedy goose gobbled up the giant pile of grains.

Which of these begin with g?

duckling   **giraffe**   **crocodile**   **geko**

What animals or objects can you think of that begin with g?

 **gap**

gas

 **pig**

dig

 **nag**

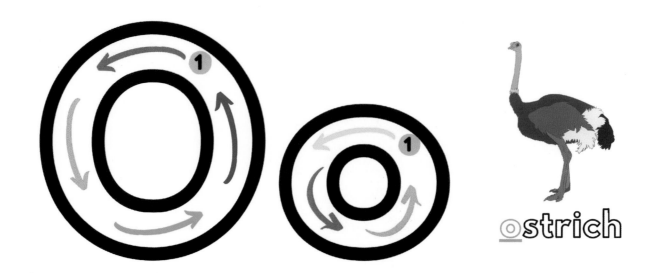

ostrich

The orange octopus sat on the seabed observing the odd world around him.

Which of these begin with o?

flounder   opossum   caterpillar   otter

What animals or objects can you think of that begin with o?

got   pot   top   dog   pop

Can you find two pairs of words that rhyme?

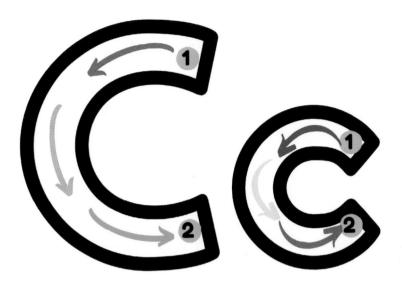

The letter 'c' makes two sounds:
soft 'c' (s sound) = when 'c' is followed by e, i or y.

 centipede

hard 'c' (k sound) = when 'c' is followed by any other letter.

camel

 **C**ertain **c**ats, like mountain **c**ats, **c**limb up **c**liffs, house **c**ats like to **c**limb up **c**urtains.

Which of these begin with c̲?

piranha   **crab**   **moose**   **coral**

What animals or objects can you think of that begin with c̲?

can   **cat**   **cot**   **cap**   **cod**

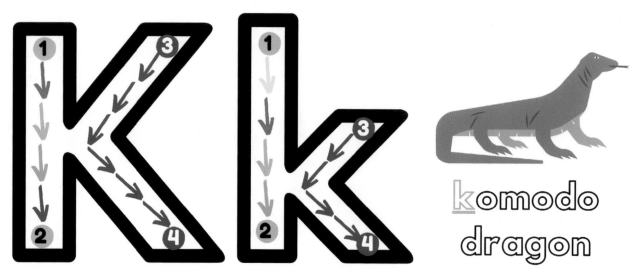

komodo dragon

Explain to your child that k makes the same sound at 'c' but 'c' is curly shaped and k looks like it is two legs kicking. Most of the time we use 'c'.

 **Female kangaroos are keen to keep their joeys (babies) in their pouch so they are close enough to kiss.**

Which of these begin with k?

horse　　　**kingfisher**　　　**bison**　　　**koala**

What animals or objects can you think of that begin with k?

 **kid**

 **kit**

 **Kim**

 **Ken**

elephant

Say the **e** sound as you follow the arrows

Electric eels use their bodies to effectively stun excited predators.

Which of these begin with e?

emperor penguins   pheasant   fly   elk

What animals or objects can you think of that begin with e?

get   pet   ten   pen   peg

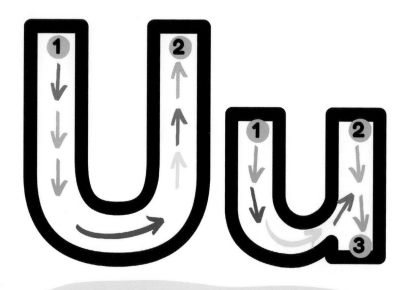

u̲mbrellabird

 **U̲naus move u̲nbelievably slowly and can be found hanging u̲nder trees.**

An unau (pronounce un/ow like in n**ow**)
is also known as a two-toed sloth.

Which of these begin with u̲?

urial   panther   red panda   porcupine

What animals or objects can you think of that begin with u̲?

run

mum

mug

cup

sun

20

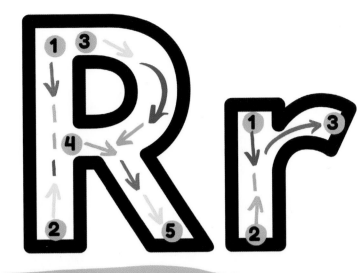

<u>r</u>abbit

<u>R</u>hinoceros have <u>r</u>ough skin, <u>r</u>ound feet and can <u>r</u>un <u>r</u>eally fast.

Which of these begin with <u>r</u>?

raccoon   sparrow   chimpanzee   guinea pig

What animals or objects can you think of that begin with <u>r</u>?

rip   rag   rat   ram   rim

Discuss words that rhyme – start by explaining that words rhyme when they have the same end sound and demonstrate this with examples: for instance, "rip rhymes with dip, ship, lip, mip…" You can inject some humour by making up words that rhyme. Ask your child to do the same and use any opportunity to do random rhyming ping-pong.

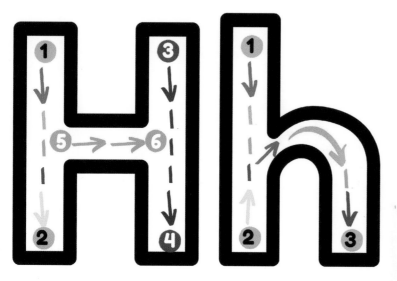

hammerhead shark

'h' is a soft sound so take care not to say "ha" when teaching it. I always think of it as more breathing out a 'h' sound rather than saying it.

 **Hawks are highly intelligent and have eye sight that is hugely better than humans.**

Which of these begin with h?

  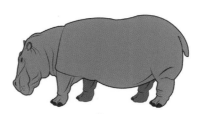 

gorilla   **hamster**   **hippopotamus**   **poodle**

What animals or objects can you think of that begin with h?

hit   **hot**   **hut**   **had**   **hug**

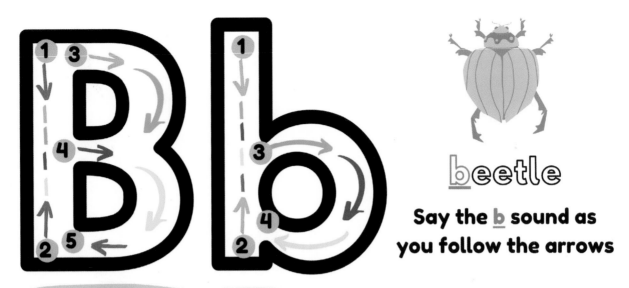

Bb

beetle

Say the **b** sound as you follow the arrows

Brown **b**ears are larger than **b**lack **b**ears **b**ut **b**oth live in **b**ig forests.

Which of these begin with **b**?

barn owl

eagle

badger

robin

What animals or objects can you think of that begin with **b**?

big

bed

bug

bus

bat

f<u>o</u>x

As with 'h', 'f' is a soft sound so make sure to model breathing it out rather than saying "fa"

 <u>F</u>lamingos have pink <u>f</u>eathers and can often be <u>f</u>ound standing on one <u>f</u>oot.

Which of these begin with <u>f</u>?

stingray   **ferret**   **mouse**   **falcon**

What animals or objects can you think of that begin with <u>f</u>?

Model using one of the words below in a sentence and ask your child to do the same. Challenge them to see if they can use more than one word in their sentence.

 **fit**
 **fin**
 **fan**
 **fog**
 **fun**

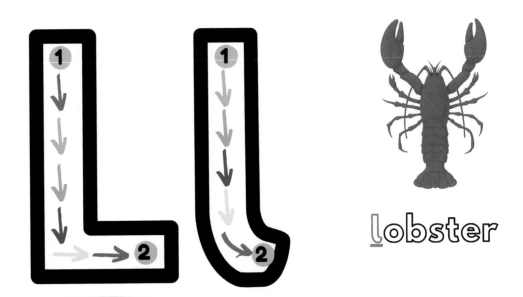

lobster

 Lemurs have long, stripy tails and like living in trees, leaping between leafy branches.

Which of these begin with l?

duck   ladybird   puffin   lynx

What animals or objects can you think of that begin with l?

let

lap

leg

bell

lot

'll' sound = 'l' sound
A double letter makes the same sound as its single letter equivalent.

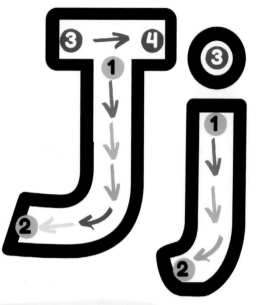

jaguar

Say the **j** sound as you follow the arrows

Jolly **j**ellyfish enjoy **j**iggling around the **j**ewelled ocean.

Which of these begin with j?

jackrabbit

sheep

chameleon

jay

What animals or objects can you think of that begin with j?

jam

jet

jog

Jill

jump

26

<u>v</u>ulture

Say the <u>v</u> sound as you follow the arrows

 <u>V</u>oles are <u>v</u>ery <u>v</u>igilant when <u>v</u>enturing out into <u>v</u>ast fields.

Which of these begin with <u>v</u>?

pelican   viper   toucan   grasshopper

What animals or objects can you think of that begin with <u>v</u>?

van   vet   vent

<u>w</u>asp

Say the <u>w</u> sound as you follow the arrows

<u>W</u>alruses <u>w</u>addle as they <u>w</u>ander around the ice and run into the <u>w</u>avy <u>w</u>ater.

Which of these begin with <u>w</u>?

wolf   cheetah   woodpecker   hedgehog

What animals or objects can you think of that begin with <u>w</u>?

web

will

wet

win

wag

28

NB - the phoneme for the letter 'q' is taught as 'qu' since 'q' is almost always followed by 'u'.

quetzal

Quokka are nocturnal. They quietly come out at night and move around very quickly.

Which of these begin with qu?

starfish   **orangutan**   **quail**   **dolphin**

What animals or objects can you think of that begin with qu?

quiz   **quit**   **quid**   **quick**

'c' sound = 'k' sound = 'ck' sound
All combinations makes the same sound.

Joint Reading and Thorny Words

There are opportunities all around us to do joint reading with our children. I will often point out simple words to my daughter on cans of food, on signs when we are out and about, and on titles of films or TV programmes. I really ramp up the praise when she reads a word which makes her feel proud and grown up. She doesn't always get it right and is not always up for reading words, so I will just demonstrate it to her, and always make it seem like a team effort when this happens. Here are some other ideas on how to incorporate 'joint reading' with your child.

Joint Stories: When reading stories, encourage your child to look at the letters they see in the title of the book and throughout the story. You can also say the sounds in different words and ask your child to blend the sounds together. Eventually, you can extend your child to read simple words such as 'dog', 'at'. You could also point out any 'tricky words' to your child (which I talk about further down the page).

Silly Word Roll: This is an extension to the 'Roll A Sound' activity. You and your child could each take three turns at rolling the dice, saying each sound you see and blending together the three sounds you land on.

= Ll
= Ee
= Ii
= Bb
= Oo
= Mm

lom   bim   obl

Thorny Words

You may know these as 'Tricky Words' or 'Sight Words'. Whatever you call them, these are words children cannot sound out but need to know by sight. I call them 'Thorny Words' as you can't touch each sound separately; you just have to look at the word and say it. See a list on page 34 of the most common thorny words your child will learn when first exposed to phonics in school.

Thorny Word Snap: Using the 'Thorny Words' cards available in the downloadable pack, play 'Snap'. It is a good idea to begin by going through all the words in the pile before beginning the game. Once you start the game, instead of saying "SNAP!" when you have a pair that matches, say the word on the cards.

the   the

I saw a big purple bug.

a   bug

Sentence Building: This activity can be used with either the 'Thorny Words' cards, 'Decodeable Words' cards, or both. You ask your child to choose one card and construct a sentence using that card. Further challenge your child by getting them to choose more than one card.

NB I have not used 'x-ray fish' as an example as it makes the 'ex' sound nor have I used 'Xylophone' as it makes a 'z' sound.

boxer dog

Arctic fox get excited when rolling around in the extremely cold snow.

What animals or objects can you think of that contain x?

 fox

 fix

mix

Max

CHALLENGE

Read these questions and answer 'yes' or 'no'

CHALLENGE

Can wax get hot?

Can a vet fix a jet?

Has a fox got six legs?

Will a dog sit in a box?

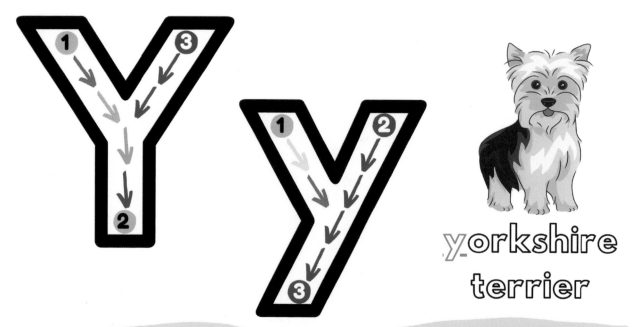

yorkshire terrier

A **y**ellow mongoose actually has orange fur and only **y**aps and **y**ells when it is scared.

What animals or objects can you think of that begin with **y**?

 **yell**

 **yak**

 **yet**

💡 Make a phonics monster/postbox/animal. Then, using sound cards create different words (or use 'tricky word' cards) and ask your child to say each sound as they pick up each card (or simply read the word with the 'tricky word' cards). Once they have blended the word together, they feed their animal or post the word.

Read these sentences

Yes! I can get a pet.

A dog can yap.

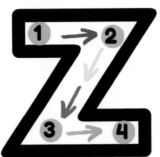

zebu bull

The zorse zoomed across the field in a zigzag pattern.

A zorse is part horse, part zebra.

What animals or objects can you think of that begin with z?

'zz' sound = 'z' sound

zap

wizz

fizz

CHALLENGE

Read these sentences and questions.

CHALLENGE

Zip it up!

Can a taxi zigzag?

Can a bell buzz?

Sound Recap

Ss   Aa   Tt   Pp   Ii   Nn

Mm   Dd   Gg   Oo   Cc

Kk   Ee   Uu   Rr   Hh

Bb   Ff   Ll   Jj   Vv

Ww   Qq   Xx   Yy   Zz

qu

Thorny Words

I	to	we	you
a	no	me	they
is	go	be	her
and	he	was	all
the	she	my	are

Glossary

Many parents may hear the word 'phonics' (and related terminology) for the first time and think 'I never learnt to read like this... what does this all mean?'. Well here is a list of the main terms you will be faced with and what they mean:

Phoneme = a single sound in a word (the sound can be made up of one letter (<u>s</u>), two letters (<u>sh</u>) or three letters (<u>igh</u>)).

Grapheme = the written letters that make up the sound i.e. 's' and 'h' for the <u>sh</u> sound.

Vowel = the letters a, e, i, o, u  I always get children to create their own 'vowel face' when teaching this

Consonant = all the other letters in the alphabet (besides a, e, i, o and u)

Digraph = two letters that make one sound e.g. *ch* in <u>ch</u>at.

Trigraph = three letters that make one sound such as *igh* in li<u>gh</u>t.

Segment = saying each sound in a word/breaking up a word into its individual sounds e.g. <u>ch</u>/<u>a</u>/<u>t</u>

Blend = merging the individual sounds together to say the word they make - so for the word 'ch/a/t', once your child said the individual sounds, they would put them together to say 'chat'.

Thorny Words = words that cannot be segmented and blended. These are also known as 'sight words' as they are words that should be read by simply looking at them such as 'the', 'no', 'into'.

Printed in Great Britain
by Amazon